"The truth will set you free,
but it will first make you miserable."

JAMES GARFIELD

To Eric, who helped me define passion, find a purpose in life, and chose to save me instead of saving himself.

TO THE READER

If you had asked me five years ago if I would live to see my 25th birthday, I would have told you, "Not likely." They say that everyone in life deserves a second chance. Five years ago I had no idea the power of another opportunity at life.

TABLE OF CONTENTS

PREFACE
MY SECOND CHANCE

On September 30, 2008 I was found guilty and convicted on Felony drug charges. The charge was the Intent to Distribute Marijuana and I was sentenced to 5 years in prison with everything suspended but 90 days and a hefty 5 years of probation with multiple stipulations. Most importantly, the honorary Judge gave me a deal that I never thought would be so important. He told me that if I completed probation fully, with no violations, he would strike the felony from my record and grant me probation before judgment.

When I stood in court that day, I didn't really care and thought I would never see the day to be free and off probation. Well, five years later, I, in fact had completed probation with no violations and on September 30th 2013 was due to go back to court.

I can stand here today and say that on January 9th 2014, I returned to court well represented by a Criminal Defense attorney and also well supported by friends and family. The Judge looked over the completed paperwork and said he would indeed strike the felony from my record and grant me probation before judgment.

I never realized how 2 minutes could instantly change your life. I am now able to vote, get a passport and most importantly, I no longer have the check the box on a job application saying I have been found guilty of a felony. I am ever so grateful to have been given this option and very thankful to all of my friends, clients and family who have supported me along the way.

This book will document my journey from felony, to fitness, to free, the choices that I made and the corresponding consequences.

THE ARREST

Cinco de Mayo 2008. I was on my way to pick up some pills. I had a broken headlight that I'd been meaning to fix for months, but hadn't gotten around to it. My one friend was sitting in the backseat of my silver Toyota Camry when the red and blue lights flashed behind us. "Oh shit," I mumbled.

I pulled over to the side of the road and fumbled for my driver's license and registration. I rolled down my window as the Police Officer shined his flashlight into the car. The smell of beer wafted out the window, hitting him in the face. "I smell alcohol in this vehicle," he said. Panic flooded my veins. My one friends' Natural Light was the least of my concerns. We were on our way to meet a hookup for some OxyContin, just enough to get me through the night and maybe the next day.

The smell of booze was enough to give the police reasonable cause to search my car. Even though the officer asked my permission, I knew I was screwed. A half pound of weed was stashed in the trunk underneath the spare tire, and $2,000 cash was hidden in the glove box...drug money.

My other buddy was sitting shotgun. He had some weed and a bowl on him. Backup officers came to assist, getting us out of the car and transported to jail. We were then handcuffed and loaded into the backs of two police cars.

I was 20 years old, not even old enough to legally drink, and was facing felony charges for distribution of marijuana and possession of paraphernalia. When we got to the Harford County Detention Center, I was stripped of my belongings and put into a holding cell. My life as I knew it, condensed to the contents of a Ziploc bag, would never be the same.

My friend who had the open container was released

right away. My other buddy and I waited for the police commissioner to find out our fate. My bail was set at five thousand dollars.

STORIES

The events of May 5, 2008 occurred five years ago. I hardly recognize that person. However, he is still there, reminding me every day that life is precious.   Each morning I recommit to living a life with purpose. It's not always easy, and there are plenty of days that I struggle with my old demons. But change isn't supposed to be easy. Commitment, willingness, and desire are necessary components for transformation... but if I can do it, anyone can.

My childhood was far from perfect, and my teenage years are the opposite of what you would think if you were to meet me for the first time now. I guess that is one of the most important lessons in life: what you see may not always reflect where someone has been...even in the darkest hour there is always a light in the distance. Although I am now fitness professional, with a personal goal of inspiring millions of people to live healthier and happier lives, there was a time in my life when I was unhappy, unhealthy, and self-destructive.

No one is perfect, and everyone has a story: our stories make us unique and take us down different paths in life. While I hope to inspire you, please do not compare your journey to mine. Just realize that we all have struggles, and we all can have hope.

BEGINNINGS

I don't really recall how my story begins...I don't remember much before age five when my dad left my mom. I was still too young to understand the consequences of their separation. In hindsight, I don't know if it would have mattered either way. Both my parents were and still are unique in their own ways. They also had different types of baggage they were carrying while trying to raise three young boys.

I was always told that there are some things in life that just aren't meant to be. Although my parents' separation was for the best, it put a damper on my early childhood, and made life difficult for my brothers, Chris and Zach, and me. When Dad left Mom, he moved into a townhouse in Perry Hall, MD. Shortly after, to make it easier on travel arrangements and finances, my mother moved to Perry Hall as well. Still clueless about what was really happening, we began to bounce between my mom's home and dad's place. Both of my parents worked full time so they had to rely on others to take care of us during the day.

My mom's parents, Yia Yia and Papou, stepped up to the plate and acted as our "daycare." It was a 20 minute drive to Yia Yia and Papou's home in the Lutherville-Timonium area. Keeping track of all our living arrangements, activities and being tossed around Baltimore County going back and forth to school, was a challenge.

Shortly after the split, my Dad began dating a new woman. They met in the Jaycees, a volunteer group they were both involved with. She lived in Iowa, but they met at a meeting in Maryland. It was really hard for me to see my Dad involved with another woman so quickly. Until this day I wonder about the timing of this relationship. When did it really start? It happened so fast!

My Dad's new woman was hard to get along with. I tried to respect her as much as I could, knowing that she was my father's new girlfriend, but I did not like her too much. As time went on, they seemed to be very happy together, got married, and moved from Perry Hall to a rural town about thirty minutes north of Baltimore called Jarrettsville. Commuting between homes, at such a distance, was a rough change. By the age of eight, I was spending one to two hours a day in the car. However, we made it work, and Jarrettsville became our new home base half of the time.

My brothers and I often joked that my Mom worked in a firehouse because I had brown hair, Chris had red, and Zach had black. During the blizzard of 1996, my stepmother was pregnant and my half- brother was born. Our new half-brother was blonde. Bopst offspring certainly covered a wide array of hair colors. I regret that Chris, Zach and I didn't develop as great of a relationship with our half-brother as we should have. His mother's personality and my father's demeanor made it difficult. The living arrangement we had growing up added to the challenge. In retrospect, I do believe that jealousy interfered as well.

TENSION BUILDS

As time went on, the tension between my Mom and Dad grew and kept spiraling like a tornado funnel, sucking and destroying everything in its path. They began to fight about custody, child support and anything else they could fight over. We would see more than ten psychologists and family therapists over the course of 5+ years. The process began to wear on us. I wasn't eating well. Maybe it was my way of coping with the divorce.

When I hit ten years of age, I began to gain noticeable weight. I was eating Pop Tarts, Cinnamon Buns, and Oreos. I turned to comfort food to make me feel better. Kids teased me in school for being overweight, and I struggled in the recreational sports, which I loved. I was embarrassed to take off my shirt at the pool, which is where we spent most of our summers growing up.

My Dad and stepmother tried to convince me to lose weight in Middle School. My Dad had me workout with a trainer as well. I was so young...I had no idea of the benefits of exercise and a healthy lifestyle. At the age of 12, I thought playing sports would keep me active enough to neutralize my weight gain, it sure worked for my friends.

I quickly came to the conclusion that I wasn't built like other preteens. I blamed my genes and my environment, instead of looking at how I could better the situation. My Mom didn't provide the healthiest meals for us growing up, and I know that played a major role in my weight gain as well. We would have cinnamon buns and sausage for breakfast, followed by pasta many nights for dinner. I really don't think Mom knew any better and was doing the best she could.

I really enjoyed growing up with Mom, and felt she was the best mother that she could be.

The more weight I gained, the more depressed I became. Insecurities grew. I was afraid to play sports, go to the pool, and even at times, go to school.

MY FOUNDATION

My brothers Chris (24), Zach (21), and I have built a bond that will never be broken. We were all very young at the time of the divorce. I was 5, Chris was 3, and Zach was a baby. It was difficult to understand why the divorce happened or what direction our lives would take. As difficult as the experience was for us, it also gifted us with the ability to grow as closely as we could, throughout the many great memories we shared.

Watching our parents fight was the roughest period. Mom and Dad refused to cooperate with each other and had trouble simply communicating. I remember at one point they would only communicate by email.

Growing up, both sets of our grandparents were our saving grace. Especially my Dad's parents, they were always there for us as kids and did everything they could to make a bad situation better.

TEENAGE YEARS

I was 13, and my Mom bought a house in the Timonium area. My commute to school was now much easier...with a change of scenery. I started at a local high school soon after, and this is where my story really gets interesting.

While dealing with all of this depression and low self-esteem, I was always looking for an escape. Normally, it was sports. I loved sports and still do to this day. I didn't enjoy playing them as much as a child because I was fat and out of shape.

One day, around age 14, I was offered to take a hit off a marijuana pipe and that is when my life really went downhill. Wow! I loved it: it took the pain away and made me happy.

Alarmingly fast, one hit led to another, then another. Soon, I began to smoke every day after school to escape the life I lived. Marijuana didn't cure my depression, but it gave me an alternative to be happy and escape the troubles I had. The more depressed I became and angry at my situation, the more my relationship with my mother suffered. There were more and more yelling outbursts, and more and more Mom and I didn't see eye to eye.

As much as I struggled with finding myself, I had a good social life. I had a lot of friends and went out quite a bit. I always wanted to have a party, since I attended so many of them and saw how much fun they were. I never really had an opportunity to do so though. Most kids threw a party when their parents were out of town. My brothers and I were never allowed to stay home when our parents were out of town. We would have to go elsewhere, often staying with other family or friends.

One day, during my junior year of high school, my mother went into the hospital for an operation. So, I decided to throw a party at her house one night while she was in the hospital. After a few hours of debauchery and loud music, a neighbor ended up calling the cops. When they showed up at the door, I ran. I wasn't necessarily scared. I mean, I knew what was going to happen before it happened. When you have a crowd of high school kids with drugs and alcohol, it is only a matter of time before the neighbors complain or become concerned, and reported you. All I wanted to do when the cops arrived was to get out of there, so I ran. After being called and coerced to return home numerous times, I finally did. I cleaned up the house and awaited the consequences of my choice from my mother. I was quickly grounded and our relationship really went south.

SOUR 16

I started smoking more weed and eventually started to sell it to support my own habit. My 16th birthday rolled around and I wanted to get high with one of my friends and go get ice cream. It was a typical "stoner" thing to do. I had to pull some weed out of my desk in my room, and I stupidly asked my brother to watch the door. Well, my mom walked right in and found out what I was doing. She called one of her friends, who was a police officer, to ask his opinion on the situation. Additionally, after a few hours, my Dad arrived.

I was kicked out of my mother's house on my 16th birthday and was forced to live with my Dad. I had no idea what to think. I had been telling Mom for the past 5 plus years how much I hated going to Dad's house. Mom kicked me out for having a little bit of pot and throwing a party. I didn't understand! I loved my mom so much. I cared for her deeply, although at times I may not have shown it.

Depression wise, being kicked out of my mother's house and being separated from my brothers put me over the edge. My mother wouldn't talk to me for a long period of time. I still don't know if she has or ever will 100% forgive me. I suppose Mom did the best she could with the situation and it was my choices that led me to this point. As I write this I understand that I really messed up and that I said things I shouldn't have said...we all make mistakes.

Not only was I kicked out of the best home I knew, I was forced to switch schools immediately and leave my friends behind. Wow! What an adjustment. I moved from a "preppy" school to a more rural school that was on a farm and had a "drive your tractor to school day." It was a very sudden and rough adjustment.

My Dad tried to restrict everything I did and treated me like a prisoner. With increased restrictions came more resentment. I would leave Dad's house and go out to party or say I was working later than I was, and party some more.

I had several jobs while living at Dad's house, including delivering pizza and washing dishes at a local restaurant. I think I worked to get away and escape from his house. I had a few jobs before being kicked out of my Mom's house but nothing serious. The more I worked, the more money I made, which simply meant I had more money to spend on pot. I was now not only selling Marijuana to support a habit, I had quickly figured out the profitability of it as well.

It wasn't long before I made friends with a similar crowd at my new school because of my obsession with weed.

Weed was my life. We would ride around for hours, and get high. We'd hike in nature parks, and do dumb stuff like eat massive amounts of junk food, and laugh constantly about nothing. As you would expect, the relationship with my Dad during this period didn't get any better. In fact, it got worse. Dad kicked me out before I was 18.

NO GRADUATION PARTY

I bounced around from acquaintance to acquaintance's couch after being kicked out of Dad's house. I eventually found a temporary residence on my friend's couch that lasted for several months, right after graduating from High School.

In spite of all the turmoil that had come to define my life, I managed to graduate from High School. I credit innate intelligence and sheer dumb luck for helping me to complete this feat. I was the only one I knew who didn't have a graduation party. That really hit home with me, but at the same time I felt like I didn't have much to celebrate at the time. Although my grades were great, I couldn't go to the colleges I wanted to due to finances. I had been accepted to East Carolina, Coastal Carolina, Salisbury and a few others.

My depression continued to worsen and my self-esteem was at an all-time low in the months following my graduation from High School. I began experimenting with Cocaine. Because of my addictive personality, it did like me. I began to abuse cocaine just as I did the marijuana and the all-nighters and benders began to become more and more frequent. Now, however, I was using the money I made in my varied revenue producing efforts to buy cocaine, and smoked all day. I also started smoking cigarettes heavily, and continued to make poor food choices. I would get stoned and eat a whole pizza and sometimes a cheesesteak sandwich as well.

The more I was selling, the more coke I snorted, and I began to get severe anxiety attacks. There was a time when I was living on my friend's couch and his mother had to take me the hospital because I thought I was having a heart attack. Sure enough, I learned my heart was fine and it was anxiety from all of the turmoil I had going on. The drugs intensified the turmoil.

I remember my friend's mom calling my parents from the hospital, chastising them for not being there for me and letting them know the situation I was in. My Mom never showed up at the hospital...my Dad came. I went home with my Dad that night and the friend that had provided my temporary couch went off to college.

I quickly enrolled in classes at Harford Community College with no idea of what to study or a career in mind. Attending Community College gave me yet another opportunity to make more drug connections and continue to waste money. I only ended up back at my fathers' house for a few days before his parents, Grandmom and Granddad, took me into their house, which was located in Hunt Valley, about 10 minutes north of where my mother lived.

I was very fortunate to be taken in by my paternal grandparents, because I had nowhere else to go. Although Grandmom and Granddad treated me like gold, I didn't do right by them. I continued to be lazy and still maintained my old drug habits.

My depression and anxiety worsened and I couldn't even smoke weed without getting a panic attack. My friends made fun of me because they really didn't understand the panic attacks. They thought I was just nuts and believe me, it was a horrifying experience. I now couldn't do the one thing I loved most anymore, get high. I also was no longer able to hang out with my friends, since getting high was all we did.

This of course brought on more anxiety and depression.

HELLO OXY

One day, I was offered a painkiller. I took it after smoking one time, and it took the anxiety away. I thought, "Wow, now I can finally smoke without anxiety", except that I now had to pop painkillers to do so. Nonetheless, this was fine by me, as I could escape reality, and get high once again.

I eventually would work my way up to a $250 a day oxycontin habit. About a year or two later, my grandparents and I agreed it was time for me "to move on". I had been sleeping until 2 or 3pm and bouncing around from job to job. I was still trying to hide the fact that I was dealing and abusing drugs.

In October of 2007, I moved into my own apartment with two of my buddies from my childhood. It's tough to support yourself making 9 or 10 bucks an hour. However, selling drugs was an easy fix to comfortably support myself. My grandparents still managed to help me by supporting me emotionally, which I was very grateful for. The relationship with my parents wasn't really there and still isn't where it should be. But I can't blame them for the current state of our relationship. The past and the mistakes I made unfortunately have defined us.

Living on your own can be tricky, as it also allows you to live with no boundaries or supervision. Here I was 19 or 20 years old and had my own apartment. The trouble is I was hiding: I really didn't like who I was or who I had become. Selling and abusing drugs allowed me to escape into another life.

Eventually, I began to do oxycontin and cocaine at the same time and that was a heart attack waiting to happen. My oxycontin habit got so bad that I couldn't wake up, eat, sleep, or live my life without being high on pills. Who would have thought these small pills could run the life of a 190 pound, 19 year old male.

The more I snorted, the sloppier my drug dealing became. I got robbed several times, but that wasn't enough to scare me into thinking about what type of consequences I could face if I maintained my path down this road. I was losing money it seemed since I was spending so much on other drugs and partying every night.

ONE HEADLIGHT

My roommates and friends began to worry about me. I was warned several times to change a headlight. I didn't pay attention or was too high to remember to do it. It was mistakes like this that eventually would lead to me hitting rock bottom.

On May 5, 2008, that day came and my hard-headedness and years of making poor choices finally caught up with me. I was in transit to completing a drug deal and was pulled over in Bel Air for having a headlight out. Little did I know, my friend in the backseat had an open container of alcohol and automatically gave the cops suspicion of mischievous behavior. The police searched my car and found ½ pound of marijuana, several thousand dollars in cash, and a scale. All I could think about was that my life was now over. What had I done? I was transported to Harford County Detention Center.

I was sitting in a jail cell handcuffed, and did nothing but think about how much money I owed my dealer, and how much of a piece of shit I must be. Sure enough, my Dad bailed me out. No matter how difficult I believed he was, I still respected him and am very thankful to him for bailing me out.

Even after that brief stay in a cell, my habits didn't change and neither did my mindset. I continued down the same path and things kept the same course. That's the root of addiction: you can't stop without help.

A strong threat was made by my drug dealer to pay him the $5,000 I owed, or else... I quickly started to look for a job with the goal of repaying that money, but since I had just been arrested it was tough and nearly impossible to find employment. After looking persistently, and scared for my life, I finally found a job at a local restaurant and began to work in the kitchen. The problem was that it only paid a little more than minimum wage and I was in debt $5,000 to someone who was threatening my life.

I had been in 19 jobs by this point in my life. Meanwhile, my brother Chris had only had one. Chris would save every penny that he could. He knew my roommates through me, and he heard about the threat that was made on my life. Chris called and asked me if I wanted him to lend me the $5,000 I owed the drug dealer. I told him not to get involved but if he really wanted to I wouldn't resist the money. He said he wanted to give it to me, and I told him I would pay him back.

Chris' actions really meant a lot and even to this day I cannot thank him enough for what he did. I took care of the debt and moved on, and swore to myself that I was done with drugs. My brothers Chris and Zach have always been my biggest supporters and I think they looked up to me. But at the time, I am not sure why. I had a history of repeatedly disappointing them both, by continually having to borrow money from them to secretly support my drug habit. After it was all said and done, I owed them both a total of around $10,000, which took a little over a year to pay off.

TEAM FELON

Besides the hefty debt I had with my brothers, I also had other more intimidating things to worry about, like going to court. I had been indicted on felony drug charges and really didn't know what that meant. I had met with several local lawyers about my case and they told me that I was more than likely going to do some jail time. Wow, I was scared...my fat ass wouldn't last in jail. All I could think about was getting beat up or butt raped.

My Dad said he had a lawyer that he knew and coincidentally my car had just blown up due to me not taking care of it. Grandmom and Granddad said they would give me money towards either a lawyer or car. Since my Dad had a lawyer for me, I went with the car. My court date was set for September 30th and I didn't really do anything to prepare for it. I didn't do any supervised classes or anything whatsoever.

On September 13th, life threw me a curveball and one of my best friends died in a car accident. It was due to drinking and driving, and I could see it coming for months. Nevertheless, I still was in a huge state of shock. I had lost 3 or 4 friends in the years past, due to similar situations, but no one as close as him. At this point, I knew I was going to go to jail. I was determined that I was going to use this devastating death to make me realize there is always a worse situation. At least I was still living. I went to my friend's funeral, as hard as it was, and deeply mourned his death as best I could.

Several weeks later, my court date arrived and I thought it was going to be postponed, but that didn't end up happening. I stood trial that day and learned I didn't have the best attorney for the situation. But, the trial went on and I was found guilty of the intent to distribute Marijuana, which is a felony. All the other miscellaneous charges were dropped. I was sentenced to 5 years in jail with everything suspended but 90 days, 5 years' probation and a hefty fine. I also had to complete 200 hours of community service and a drug education program. My first thought was "I should have taken my grandparent's offer of money to hire a lawyer and not spent it on a car!" I often wonder where I would be if I had chosen to use the money that my grandparents offered me to hire a high-class lawyer instead of using it to buy a car. After all, it was my sentence that changed me...

The judge gave me 3 weeks to report to jail and told me that if I could complete my probation without any mess-ups or violations, that he would strike the felony from my record. All I could think of was that there was no way in hell that I was going to be able to do that.

Team Felon: I now had a title, "felon", that I thought would define and haunt me for the rest of my life. My existence had definitely hit rock bottom at this point. I had no sense of direction. I didn't know what I wanted to do in life and even questioned why I existed.

JAIL

On October 21, 2008, about a week after my 21st birthday, I reported to the Harford County Detention Center. From the minute I stepped into the lobby and the door closed behind me, I was so scared. I am sure people think that 90 days isn't too bad. Imagine having your freedom taken away for that period of time, not being able to see anyone, eat the food you want, or even talk to whom you want. Guards watching you to make sure you were on your best behavior and no mistakes were made. If you acted up, they could take away your freedom for longer or send you into solitary confinement. I was trapped inside a box, and had no way out.

For a guy, not seeing any girls was also tough, and the food was far from world class. We would have meals such as diced mice and rice (rice with chopped up mystery meat), and vegetables or sweaty meat sandwiches, as we would call them. We didn't know exactly what they were or what the meat was made out of. The best meal in jail happened to be on Thanksgiving. My sentence was timed such that I would spend Thanksgiving and Christmas in jail.

After checking in at the front desk, I was put in a holding cell or "bullpen" until they decided where I was going to be placed more permanently. I ended up being placed into a dorm with dozens of other criminals. I was so terrified that all I wanted to do was cry. I didn't know what to expect. You hear all of these horror stories about the things that happen in jail. I was afraid I was going to get beat up, stabbed and/or ridiculed.

I stayed in this unit for a day or two, and then was transferred to a different unit. This is the unit where I would meet a guy who played a major role in helping me make the decision to change my life.

My head was so out of whack when I first got to jail, people said I reminded them of a zombie. I would walk around with my head down and just had no idea what was going on. All I would do is think and think and think. I would cry wondering what my life was going to be like and if I was going to live past 30. I had no idea that it could get better.

ERIC

Eric had been in a drug abuse situation similar to mine. The difference was that Eric had been incarcerated for almost 10 years and was in the detention center on a detainer waiting to go to court. He had dozens of felonies on his record for burglaries and other criminal offenses.

Eric quickly invited me to play scrabble with him and a few

other guys. I shared my story with everyone that asked and they had a lot of respect for me for what had happened and thought I got a bad break.

Eric and I talked about why I had gotten to this point, and he kept me positive. He advised me not to worry about the things I couldn't control. I continued to play scrabble with the guys and surprisingly, ended up becoming great at it! However, I still continued to think negatively about my future. I was very worried that I was not going got make it in the real world once I was released from jail and I was going to let everyone down. I had a strong history of failures and didn't think this time would be any different.

I quickly noticed that Eric would work-out for around 3 hours a day. He was a machine, doing crazy stuff you see in YouTube videos. Eric was jacked. He told me that after giving me a few weeks to adjust to being in jail he was going to get me to workout. I pretty much told him he had a better chance of winning the mega millions.

Eric had bugged me for weeks to exercise and told me how much better I would feel. I decided to make a change and let him train me. As resistant as I was, I had no idea what I had gotten myself into. He had me get on the ground to perform pushups and I couldn't even hold myself up to even go down. I tried again, but from my knees. I couldn't even do that. Forget running, I couldn't even walk for a minute or two without being winded. I was so out of shape!

All of the drugs and cigarettes consumed in my prior years had taken a toll on my body and lungs. Not to mention I was around 190 pounds, and if I had to guess, about 40% body fat. I could have been a model for Pillsbury. Just call me the Pillsbury Doug Boy!

That first workout was an embarrassment to me and I

knew something had to give. Eric put me on a diet, which didn't seem too bad considering the food in jail tasted god-awful. Grandmom and Granddad would send me money for commissary, which is a store where you could buy other food items such as Ramen Noodles, Fruit Snacks, Candy, etc. I was very fortunate to continue to have their support. They were the only ones besides Chris and Zach who were really there for me.

So after a few days of working out I started to see some improvements. I could do a "girl" pushup and could walk a bit longer. I set a goal that I wanted to be able to do 10 pushups by the time my sentence was over. The workouts were tough and I doubted myself a lot. I reminded myself to never give up and to keep going. Every time I wanted to quit, I would think about the things that motivated me to do better, such as the way my parents treated me.

Eric was awesome at keeping me fired up. He would never let me quit and brought the best out in me. His words of wisdom stuck with me throughout the sentence, and in my life today. I always wondered why he chose me or why he did this, but I am blessed I was the one he picked to help. I think he could see it in me, he could see the boy who was trapped. After speaking to me, he knew I was no dummy and that I could have goals in life. I just didn't know how to break through the walls of the Doug that I didn't like.

MIND CHANGE

I continued to work-out with Eric despite the daily struggle. About a few weeks later, my Dad and brothers came to visit me. By this time, my mind had started to change. I was feeling more positive with the small improvements I saw from working out, and I actually felt I was going to make it. One hard thing about being locked up is when you would receive letters from friends and family. They would say various things about how they were worried about me, missed me and hoped that I could make it when I got out.

I remember looking at my Dad and my brothers that very same day. All my Dad did was yell at me. I walked out of the visitor's room and wondered why he thought yelling at me was going to make me feel good...I was in jail! I was so angry. My Dad was yelling at me because he didn't believe that I was going to make it after jail without rehab. This is one of the struggles that I had to deal with.

I then walked back into the jail unit and said to Eric "lets workout." He looked like I had just told him something he never thought he would hear. I worked out harder than ever that day. He was asking what was up. He could tell I was upset. I told him what happened during my father's visit and I quickly learned that my parents' lack of belief in my ability to succeed would be the fuel for my life change.

It took several months before my Mom even came to see me. The thing with her is that whenever I needed her the most, she was rarely there for me.

Still in jail, my workouts were booming and I was seeing some significant changes in my mind, body and soul. I was happier, smiling again, and knew I was going to make it upon my release! Everyone in jail was pulling for me to make it and my self-confidence grew exponentially.

MATH

Every day I would do the math for when I would be released and finally I was told I would be released on December 26, 2008. After talking to several jail mates, I learned the reason why many inmates don't survive after being released following a jail sentence is because they don't know how to adjust to being in the real world. In jail, everything is taken care of for you as far as housing, food, showers, etc. I was very anxious to see what it would be like to be free again.

The day quickly came for my release. Believe it or not, I actually cried the day I left jail. After a rough start, I had adjusted and made a lot of friends, and had times I will never forget. Eric is someone I will always remember. He was dedicated to change me and help me make the decision to make the most out of my second chance at life. I didn't know how I would ever repay him since he was still locked up, and had yet to go to court for another sentencing.

By the time of my release, I had reached my goal of doing 10 pushups and I was able to run 2 miles! I also had lost around 15 pounds, but most importantly my mindset had changed. I had reached some personal goals, felt more confident and my self-esteem was much better. I was 21 years old and for the first time in my life, I had a sense of direction. I knew I was going to continue to change, not only for my family and myself, but also for Eric. He put so much time and effort into helping me throughout my sentence.

Eric gave me a workout routine before I left, which I still keep in my car as a good luck charm. He wrote on there "remember you are no longer a fat ass and don't have to be one again..." Those words meant and still mean the world to me.

Jail time taught me lessons about life and about respect. In jail, you had to respect one another or you would be disliked or possibly beaten up. Jail also taught me not to take things for granted in life, and to be thankful for what you have. Above all, I learned to recognize that freedom was a privilege. My freedom is the one thing I took for granted and it bit me in the butt.

My name was called for my release, and after having an

emotional goodbye with the members of my cell unit I walked into the lobby and changed into the clothes I wore when I reported to jail a few months before. I walked outside into freezing cold weather wearing shorts and a polo shirt. There was snow on the ground. I didn't even think to plan ahead! Oh well!

I swore I would stop smoking cigarettes, but one of the first things I did was buy a pack. On a very positive note though, I was still focused on being drug free, and keeping up with my daily workouts.

FREEDOM

It felt so great to be free! I wanted to do things I never would have wanted to do in the past, like go to the Aquarium and the Zoo. I still thought about Eric, and everything he did for me. I swore to myself that every opportunity I had to change someone's life, I would. I wanted to pass the torch along per say.

My next step after being released was to find a place to live and my grandparents said I could stay with them upon their return from a cruise. I still had around 10 days to find somewhere to sleep. My Mom wouldn't let me stay with her, and I didn't want to stay with my Dad, so I bounced around friends' homes for a few days before my grandparents returned.

My friends and their families provided places to stay, money, and most importantly, moral support. Shortly after being released, I met with parole and probation. They introduced me to my Probation Officer and informed me of all the stipulations. These included a monthly payment of around $90 a month, reporting as directed, random urinalysis, and getting permission to change jobs or leave the state.

Around the same time, my grandparents returned from their cruise and I moved in with them. They established some ground rules that I agreed to. One of the biggest was for me to get a job. Being a convicted felon, that was one hard thing to do. I pounded the pavements for months filling out applications left and right. I had a long resume, I had 19 jobs, but I was only 21! Holding a job wasn't a strong suit in the past, but I was determined to use the lessons I learned to change that. After a few months, I finally got a job at a local liquor store, Ridgeley Wines and Spirits. At first, I was nervous thinking I shouldn't be around alcohol all day. I soon realized how horrible alcohol would be for me, as I watched some customers come in at 9 in the morning desperate to purchase their bottle of cheap vodka.

During the job hunt, I also enrolled at Rock State Park to complete my mandatory community service. The tasks varied from cutting grass, shoveling snow, and cleaning toilets to even picking bamboo. It took me about a year to complete the 200 hours and I managed to make the best of it.

I also had enrolled in a First Step Drug Education program, which I completed flawlessly.

GYM TIME

I continued to work out, but I didn't have a gym membership, so all I did was run and do the pushup routine Eric gave me. I continued to eat healthy, but not nearly enough. I lost another 20 lbs. or so, although I still had doubts about myself when I was working out and wanted to quit at times. I always remembered how far I had come and not how far I had yet to go. The internal words of motivation would be a huge positive factor in my journey.

I joined a local gym, but after working out for a few months, I hired a personal trainer. I knew I needed some guidance to help get me to the next level. My friend's boyfriend was a trainer and I started with him that week. We would train a few days a week, and he gave me a modern meal plan and an exercise routine I could use in the gym. I followed it diligently and lost another 25 lbs.! I was in the best shape of my life and felt amazing!

My grandparents noticed a big difference in my personality, mood and depression. The depression was non-existent and my anxiety had gone away! I wish I had known the benefits of exercise long before, but I don't know if I would be where I am today without experiencing all that I did.

I was still smoking cigarettes, but managed to make improvements in endurance. My goal for that summer was to run my first 5k, and I was going to stop smoking after the day of the 5k. I slowly weaned my way down to 2 cigarettes a day. I didn't want to stop smoking before the race, because I knew what it was like the first time and didn't want the lungs to have to readjust. I called my Mom and Dad and asked for their support running the 5K. My Mom was MIA, but my Dad showed up. I ran the 5k and finished in 23:04. I was so proud of myself! The next day I quit smoking and I haven't touched one cigarette since.

 I continued to work at the liquor store and actually held this job for more than a year! I was promoted to a shift supervisor, and was responsible for overseeing the store clerks and was in charge while the manager was not there.

The more I exercised, the more passionate I became about health and fitness. I was always an "all or nothing" kind of person. I rarely missed a healthy meal or workout.

In November of 2009, I decided it was time to exercise on my own. I went to the Maryland Athletic Club and Wellness Center for a tour and to inquire about membership. I was offered a $60 for 60 Days program called the Healthy Start Program. It is designed for new exercisers to jump-start them into a gym setting. I decided to take it and began working out there. I loved the MAC with its pools, basketball courts, and very nice weights!

After the Healthy Start Program, I didn't continue my membership at the MAC due to my tight budget. Instead, I worked out with my friends at a local gym that was $10 a month. It wasn't nearly as nice and the staff members weren't as helpful as those as I had met at the MAC, but it gave me a cheap place to exercise.

I really wanted to give back some of the lessons I learned and help my current circle of friends with their health and wellness goals.

DEEP LOSS

In early 2010, my Papou died from a heart attack. He had had many health problems before his death, including several strokes and a leg amputation. Around the same time, my Yia Yia developed Alzheimer's disease. She too died later that year. That was a tough year for my family, most of all for my mother.

I was saddened deeply by the loss of my maternal grandparents and will be forever grateful for the role they played in my life. I wish they would have had an opportunity to meet the new, healthy Doug.

MAC Employee

In October of 2010, I pursued a job opening at the Maryland Athletic Club and Wellness Center as a fitness specialist, with hopes of becoming a certified personal trainer. I wanted to be in a position to inspire others to change their lifestyle.

I was selected for an interview and came in and met with Helen, the Manager of the MAC's Hunt Valley location. After the interview, all seemed well and I thought I was going to be hired on the spot. But, I wanted to be honest with her and let her know my story and about my past. I told her about the felony and how it had changed my life. I begged her to hire me and told her that if she didn't hire me she would be making a mistake. After undergoing further questions from the human resources department and from Helen, I WAS HIRED! I thought the floor was going to break in my grandparents' house I was so excited!

I now had to give notice to the liquor store. Out of the 20 jobs that I had, this was the first place of employment that I left on my own terms. They were understanding about my departure and wished me luck.

I had never been so fired up about a job before in my life. I was happy to work! I think back and I could never imagine putting those words in the same sentence. My role as a Fitness Specialist was to provide hospitality to the members and help them get started on the machines we had. But most importantly, we help the members set goals for their health and wellness.

After filling out the paperwork and undergoing a few weeks of training, I began to think about how I was going to get certified as a trainer. I went to the MAC'S main location in Timonium to exercise regularly. I introduced myself to a few of the employees there and told them I was a new fitness specialist at the "MAC Express" as it's called, since it's a smaller location.

One of the employees I clicked with was Billy. He invited me to try his boot camp and by watching him train, I could tell he knew what he was doing. So I started to ask him questions everyday about how to become a trainer. He gave me the names of a few organizations and I decided to buy the books for the NSCA-CPT (National Strength and Conditioning Association). I studied diligently while I was working the front desk as well as at home.

I then began to pick Billy's brain about how he built his business. He was kind enough to share all of his tips, and fortunately I believed everything he said. I kept bugging him when I had questions and he was always kind enough to answer. He helped build the business that I have today.

I am very thankful to have met Billy. He is passionate, delivers outstanding customer service and is a great trainer. He told me some of his clients had been with him for 6 or 7 years, so I knew he was doing something right. After studying for several months, I felt I was ready to take the NSCA-CPT test.

On March 31, 2011, I went to take the NSCA-CPT test at a testing location about 30 minutes away from the facility I worked at. I was so nervous and worried I was going to fail. But, I passed and started training gym members in April.

After listening to Billy's lessons and guidance, I quickly built my training business. I felt I had a special gift to share with others with the story I had. I loved connecting with members and learning their stories and how I could help them improve their lives. Billy always taught me to make the customer feel that you are helping them, and that they are not helping you.

Everyone has a story and it's about using your story to connect with others and build lasting relationships. It took me a while to share my entire story with clients, worrying about what they would think.

I became a full time trainer in 4 months but I wasn't yet satisfied. That's the magnificence of passion; it drives one to continually set higher goals for oneself. I am always eager to learn how to master my craft. I continued to ask Billy how I could do better and become a top trainer in the company. He gave me more advice and tips and I used that to continue to grow.

My grandparents were so proud of me. It was rewarding to know that I finally gave them what they had deserved. But more importantly, I began to believe that I was living the life that I deserved, one full of purpose and meaning.

In June, I decided it was time to move out of my grandparents' house. I was much more financially stable and mature than the previous apartment experience, and it was time to move on. I moved into an apartment about 2 miles away from the MAC Express with a lady, Jan, who worked there as well.

TRAINING TIM

In August of 2011, I began to train Tim, who was one of the founders of the MAC. He was a client of a previous trainer who had left and I decided I would take him on following her departure. I was nervous, all I could think about was what would happen if I hurt him or if he passed out. But Tim was down to earth and didn't even act like he owned the place. We built a great relationship through the personal training and by sharing the workplace life.

I met Liz, Tim's wife, and co-owner of the MAC. Like Tim, she is very passionate about the industry and a pleasure to work for. They both serve as mentors to me with my business and personal life. Their mission as a company is to help others get healthy and fit on time or ahead of time. That really hit home with me, since they cared about helping people become better, just as I did.

My personal training business continued to grow, and in October of 2011, I began to start to teach a TRX class. TRX is a form of suspension training designed by a Navy Seal. This is where I met Maria, our Corporate and Medical Liaison for the MAC whom I had taken a few TRX classes with before I was a trainer. She seemed to enjoy my class and would refer me people left and right.

As time went on, Maria and I became really close. She was one of the first people I had told at the MAC about my past. This is because I was still slow to openly share my past in volumes due to the fact that I was still a convicted felon.

People hear that term felon, and they cringe. I didn't want to risk losing clients or friends by telling them my story. Nevertheless, I quickly realized that if people lost respect for me because of my past and were too judgmental or narrow-minded to appreciate what I had accomplished, then they weren't the right people to surround and support me.

MARIA

That November, Maria invited me over for Thanksgiving dinner. At first, I was not going to go. Not because I didn't like Maria, I thought she was awesome. But, I didn't want to feel like a misfit and be a burden to her family. After some thought, I decided to accept the invitation, and I am glad that I did. It was the best Thanksgiving I had ever had. I met Maria's three daughters, Katie, Maria, and Caroline. Katie and Maria and I went to the Ravens' home football game together that night. We got lost on the way home and we all started fighting and seriously screaming at each other. As awkward as it was, it made us all closer and was a great way to break the ice. Katie and Maria shared with me how happy their mom was that I came to dinner. Maria always treated me well, brought the best out in me and made me feel welcome. Maria selflessly filled a void in my life and still serves as my "go to" person for advice on anything.

Maria had bought her daughters, Maria and Katie, several training sessions with me for Christmas the previous month. They were both home from college for about a month and wanted to use the time to kick start into a routine. I began training them both around the second week of January. As I do with all of my clients, I sat Maria and Katie down for a consultation and talked to them about why they needed me or why their goals were important to them. They both had different goals and had come from a divorced family, and they each had their own story. Katie and I found out through working together that we had a lot in common and we became really close. I still maintained contact with her sister, Maria, and stayed focused on addressing the sisters' individual needs.

Maria and Katie were both so different in many ways, but they shared one trait: both had hearts the size of a boulder. The one I really was able to help the most was Katie. She was not at all happy with where she was with her health. She informed me of her terrible eating habits and how she had a history of yo-yo dieting. After talking to her, I found out that she had Lyme disease when she was younger and it caused her to be inactive for quite some time. I told her that together, we were going to help the situation and improve her quality of life.

I will never forget the first time Katie and I worked out together and she had to hold my hand to do a simple lunge. From then on, I wanted to help this girl and realized I was going to have to give it a 110% effort to do so. We put together a plan for the next month while she was home. She lost about 25 pounds during her first 4 weeks of the lifestyle change. Katie was committed to the process and ended up losing a total of 65 lbs. Most importantly, Katie helped change her own life. Her relationships and self-confidence greatly improved. Helping Katie meant so much to me. I don't know if it was because of what her mother had done for me or if it was out of the passion I had for helping others. Perhaps it was a combination of both feelings.

TEAM BOPST AND A NEW "HIGH"

Right after Thanksgiving, I began to do some research on trainers around the world who had made a name of themselves. The one that stood out to me was Todd or TD as we call him, who trained in San Diego. I learned that Todd trained many world class athletes and had a heavy involvement with TRX and Under Armour. I remember watching one of his YouTube videos and his energy was off the charts. I was like "how does he do it???". The answer was simple: passion!!!

I began reading Todd's blogs and following him on Facebook. From reading the things Todd said and listening to Billy, I learned that if you treat your clients well, they will treat you well in return. Around the holidays, Todd posted useful information about how to improve client retention. One of his suggestions was to host a holiday party for your clients. So I did just that and crammed about 15-20 people into my apartment one night for a little get together. Everyone had a great time and it was definitely a hit.

Later on that month, I circled back with Billy and we were preparing for my first "full year" as a trainer. I told him about my goal of becoming one of the top trainers in the company and he was helping me plan out my year. I continued to follow Todd throughout the rest of 2011 and in 2012 my business improved by 67%! I had gone from revenue of $6,000 in December of 2011 to $10,000 by January of 2012. I learned though, you must be humble in this industry. A high ego will lead to nothing but selfish actions and decisions. In the fitness industry, it's expected to have about a 20% attrition rate due to the nature of the business. I wanted to find anyway I could to continue to strive to deliver exemplary customer service to my clients.

With the help of a client, we branded my business with the name "Team Bopst." I wanted to let my clients know that all who trained with me at the MAC were part of a bigger family. We were a team, "Team Bopst", and not just a trainer and a client. Being part of a group added extra accountability among the "team" and allowed the clients to get to know each other.

The brand quickly grew and I got wristbands and t-shirts made with the slogan "inspired to perspire." I wanted to inspire my clients, just as they inspired each other and me. I love all of my clients, they inspire me with their unique stories, and I am very thankful to be in a business where I can touch and be enriched by so many lives on a daily basis.

Helping others identify and accomplish life-changing goals quickly became a new "high" for me. It's amazing how you can go from thinking a perfect day is snorting an 8 ball of coke, snorting 3 80's of oxycontin, and smoking ¼ ounce of weed, to being pumped up knowing you've improved someone's life and helped them get better.

SEEKING BALANCE

One of the hardest things about this job is being able to balance your life. It's part of the business and par for the course. Business was still doing well, but I was burning out. I was working sometimes day and night, delivering 40+ personal training sessions a week. I was giving so much on a daily basis and it became habitual. But I chose this career path, and love what I do as a fitness professional.

I take pride in making sure that I a highlight in my clients' day. But, even though things were going well, and I was burning out, I was eager to learn about how to manage my time better while continuing to grow my brand and business.

I applied for the Todd's Mentorship Program in April of 2012. I was accepted and was stoked for the opportunity to learn from the best. All training activities were located at his top rated gym, Fitness Quest 10 in San Diego, CA. You would think since a trainer extraordinaire operates it, we would be doing nothing but working out and learning cool new exercises right? Wrong!

We learned about life and discovering what our purpose was. I was surrounded with 25+ fitness pros from all over the world including Guatemala, Canada, Scotland and various parts of the States. We shared a lot of great information with each other, and still keep in touch. At the end, it got emotional as we planned out the things we wanted to accomplish in the next 90 days, the year, five years and for LIFE. Things many of us never had thought about.

We also discussed the barriers and obstacles that were getting in the way of our business and I listed mine. The things I had to change were getting rid of the negativity that I was surrounding myself with including some people from my past as well as demons I still had inside from years back. I needed to start to put myself first in many ways I wasn't doing. The last thing we had to do was write our life decree, which was pretty much an exercise that documents what you want to be remembered for when you die. Now this could change over the years, but at the time here is what it read:

LIFE DECREE

Now this could change over the years, but at the time here is what it read:

"Thank you Lord and to the law for giving me a second chance in this journey called life. Without you, I would have overdosed or been killed in some other way much sooner. I'm so grateful that Eric picked me off the ground in jail and began the transformation of a new beginning. Exercise and a healthy lifestyle changed my life and allowed me to find true passion and purpose for life on earth. Helping people get better every day and sharing my story gave me a new feeling of being high. I inspired thousands day in and day out by leading by example, inspiring, and practicing what I preached. I am blessed I was able to impact the lives of so many youths before it was too late. I proved to them through a powerful story that anything can be done through hard work and dedication. I am so grateful to have had Grandmom and Granddad, you were the best grandparents anyone could ask for and without you I would never have made it. You gave me a home and saved me from living in my car on even worse on the streets. Chris and Zach, you guys were incredible brothers to me. Fred, I am super proud of where you are today and hope we can continue to grow our relationship. We had a bond no one could break and we went through so much together that no matter how far we were from each other we were always so close. I loved you guys so much. Mom and Dad I also loved you guys so very much. We had many good memories and hope you are proud of who I have become and respect me for the choices I made. I would also truly like to thank the MAC, they gave me the chance I needed and opened the door for me to rise and shine as I was intended to. I cannot thank the MAC enough for the opportunity to carry out my mission of inspiring people to greatness. But mostly, the MAC gave me the opportunity to meet Maria. We quickly grew close because of our shared passion and purpose, and quickly she made me part of her family. Maria and the girls, I am so blessed, and thankful that I was made part of your family. Although I was a late addition, I think some things are better late than never. It's okay though, I'm in a better place now. Although

I'm not here physically, please remember my legacy as my transformation from a nearly dead at a young age, fat, depressed drug dealer, to someone who inspired greatness in himself and others every day. Also having a special gift to make people laugh and feel better...I truly was the highlight of everyone's day. As much as I know I didn't take care or think of myself as much as I should have, I would never trade that in place of having the ability to touch the hearts and lives of so many people on a regular basis.

Doug

LIFE GOES ON

Upon my return from the mentorship, I was so fired up and eager to use the tools I learned in San Diego. I quickly joined Todd's Mastermind Institute program to keep up with all of Todd's words of wisdom. I did my best to eliminate the negativity in my life and to try to take more care of myself. I did okay for a while, but still struggled with the taking care of myself part.

A little over a month later, Maria invited me to go on their annual family retreat to Williamsburg, and go to Busch Gardens. I couldn't wait to go. I was nervous because every time I traveled I had to get permission from my probation officer to leave the state and it always brought back the memories of the past. I did get permission, and we had such a great time! It was the first "family" vacation I had been on in nearly a decade. It felt great to relax and be myself. We enjoyed each other's company and shared many laughs including watching me eat a rare funnel cake and turkey leg at the amusement park!

When I got back, it was business as usual and I continued to follow the guidance of Todd and his Mastermind program. I started to really talk about how much of an impact it was having on my career with Liz and Tim. I showed them the things I learned at the mentorship, as well as what I was currently learning in the Mastermind Program. I ended up wowing them so much with the work of Todd, that they booked to have him out to speak to our trainers in late fall of that year.

October quickly rolled around and I was turning 25! Maria and her daughters had me over for a party and decorated the house lime green, since that was the "Team Bopst" theme color. It is things like that that continue to really make me appreciate Maria and her family, my family. It's the little things in life that we often are guilty of taking for granted.

A few weeks later, I was invited to the "Mastermind Institute Retreat" at Fitness Quest 10 in San Diego. There were only 4 of us that were able to go and we did some serious "brainstorming" and "masterminding." It was yet another fantastic experience and I learned again that my biggest struggle was taking care of myself. While my training career was steady, I wasn't fulfilling myself. I had a sub-par social life and was still burning out.

I wanted to elevate myself from a "trainer" to more of a well-rounded fitness professional. I wanted to establish myself like Todd. Well, that task is a lot easier said than done! Todd and I connect well, and I look up to and value him as a mentor. He is real and has been in my shoes before as a "grunt" working trainer and transformed himself into one of the most recognized fitness professionals in our industry. His coaching program has had such a tremendous impact on my life. You spend so much time holding others accountable as a personal trainer that you often forget to hold yourself accountable. Todd's program makes you elevate your game to be accountable to yourself and teammates.

PASSING THE TORCH

After my endeavor in jail, I really wanted to pass on the torch that my cellmate Eric had given me. As I write this book, I feel that I have! Having a personality that involves being so eager to give and help others is great and rewarding. It can also be negative in that you get yourself in too deep helping others and you neglect yourself.

Inspiring others is all about finding any way to show you care and using that to connect with each other. That is why I think I have had success as a trainer. I am able to connect with our customers, and let them know that I have been there. Many assume that all trainers have been fit for life and live happily ever after. It is definitely not the case. We all work hard, but can also struggle at times to stay healthy.

In November of 2012, there was an opening to the "platinum" level of Todd's mastermind group. This would be a significant upgrade. I now would be on a "team" with 25+ other fitness pros to hold each other accountable. Each team has a coach and live calls each month to follow up on the ins and outs of our businesses. I am very fortunate to have been accepted into this elite group. It has single handedly helped change my mindset on my business. Our coach Kelli, assisted by the rest of our teammates, does an incredible job at making sure we are at the top of our game.

In December of 2012, it was already time for the second annual "Team Bopst" Holiday Party. The "team" had nearly doubled since the previous year, so one of my clients offered to have the party at her house. What a thoughtful gesture! We had about 35-40 people show up and I was so proud to have as much support from my clients as I did. Tim and Liz also attended, which really meant a lot to me, and reinforced they were in my corner. It is rewarding to know that the owners of the place you work are so supportive of you.

Christmas that year was great and relaxing. Got to see my parents, brothers and also spent some time with Maria and her family as well.

STAYING HUMBLE

We had our annual MAC all-staff meeting at the beginning of 2013. This is where they announce where we are as a company and reassess the previous year and go over goals for the next. It is also when they announce the top-producing trainers in the company. After much hard work and dedication, I was named the #1 producing trainer at the MAC. I had reached my goal.

As much as I was proud and honored, I began to think, "where is this going to get me?" "Do I really want to be just a trainer?" "What does #1 mean?" I had some new goals. I have learned as a trainer that ego will be your worst enemy, and wanting to be the #1 trainer had nothing but ego written all over it.

So...my goals for 2013 changed. I wanted to be able to inspire others on a whole other level! I decided I wanted to take a bigger role in helping other trainers build their business, I wanted to write a motivational book and I wanted to speak more! I still wanted to train, but I also wanted to tackle these other goals.

After talking to a few coworkers and Todd, we decided "From Felony to Fitness to Free" was the most suitable and eye catching title for the book. I went with it and planned to start writing in the spring of 2013.

I had always wondered how I was going to repay Eric. I saw him a few times after he was released from prison, and even kept up with him working out. However, Eric went back to prison shortly after for a reason I am not even sure of. I still wanted to repay him, but couldn't help him physically. Eric chose not to help himself, but to help me...I wanted to honor him by helping others who choose to help themselves like I did. People often ask why I do some things or why I want to help others so much. You may also ask, why don't you put yourself first? It's all because of Eric and what he did for me in jail. I also honor Eric by dedicating this book to him, wherever he may be.

ABRIDGMENT

My journey is not yet over, it has only just begun, and the story will keep going. I'd like to help encourage hope in someone else's journey, and inspire them to write their own story so that they can one day do for others as I have done for them. Without Eric, I would never have written this book, become a fitness professional, or even transformed my life. Not a day goes by that I don't wonder where I would be in life if Eric hadn't made the decision to care. It keeps me motivated to keep caring and putting others first. I hope one day we reunite so he can see how far I really have come since those days in jail.

Life has taken a complete 180 since that fateful Cinco de Mayo in 2008. I have been drug free for six years and have found a passion and career in fitness. Most importantly, the way I feel about myself has dramatically improved. My depression and anxiety are gone and for the first time, I have a sense of purpose and belonging in life. As for my family and friends, I only surround myself with the ones who bring the best out in me and continue to help me grow. Whether they are blood or not, I have learned I work best when I am surrounded by champions. As for my mother and father, the relationships have come a long way since and continue to get better.

Coincidentally, my relationship with my family is better

now than it ever has been. We respect each other and I can tell they are proud of where I am today. My half-brother has turned out to be a great kid and a super athlete. I wish him the best of luck. I really need to thank my grandparents especially; they were my #1 cheerleaders from the beginning. No matter what the circumstances were, they always were there to help me with whatever I needed. I am forever indebted to them. I am also very proud of where Chris and Zach are today. They have been such great supporters and have grown up so fast. Without them, childhood would have been impossible to survive.

PROLOGUE

If you read my pages and are struggling and wondering how my story relates to yours, it does! Sure I was in jail and didn't have any freedom, but the light bulb still had to click. I could have sat in my cell for the entire sentence and done nothing but sleep. With the help of Eric, I decided to make the decision to change.

Every day we are faced with choices that will have an impact on our lives. I chose to use drugs to contend with my stress. Because of that choice, I ended up arrested and lost a chunk of my life. My brothers were in the same situation and made better choices. While I was in jail, I chose to begin to workout and not continue to mope around pondering where I was in life. It's a choice we make to exercise and eat healthy every day. Each day we are fortunate enough to make these choices that can turn negatives into positives.

I wrote this book to inspire you and give you hope that you can do it too! There were so many times I was ready to quit and surrender to this journey we call life. You have to dig deep and keep fighting! You have to remember how far you have come and not how far you have to go! Todd once said, "Live a life worth telling a story about...what's your story?"

This is my story and I wanted to share it to help you answer this fundamental question: "What is your story going to be?"

FROM FELONY

at my lowest low

TO FITNESS

personal training at The MAC

TO FREE

the day my felony charge
was striked from my record

Made in the USA
Middletown, DE
01 November 2019